10-minute

SEASONAL
CRAFTS
for
WINTER

ANNALEES LIM

WINDMILL
BOOKS
New York

Published in 2015 by Windmill Books, An Imprint of Rosen Publishing
29 East 21st Street, New York, NY 10010

Senior Editor for Wayland: Julia Adams
Craft stylist: Annalees Lim
Designer: Emma Randall
Photographer: Simon Pask, N1 Studios

Photo Credits: All step-by-step craft photography: Simon Pask, N1 Studios; images used throughout for creative graphics: Shutterstock.

Library of Congress Cataloging-in-Publication Data

Lim, Annalees, author.
 10-minute seasonal crafts for winter / by Annalees Lim.
     pages cm. — (10-minute seasonal crafts)
 Includes index.
 ISBN 978-1-4777-9218-6 (library binding) — ISBN 978-1-4777-9219-3 (pbk.) —
 ISBN 978-1-4777-9220-9 (6-pack)
 1. Handicraft—Juvenile literature. 2. Winter—Juvenile literature. I. Title. II. Title: Winter.
 TT160.L48495 2015
 745.5—dc23
                              2013048372

Manufactured in the United States of America

CPSIA Compliance Information: Batch #WS14WM: For Further Information contact Windmill Books, New York, New York at 1-866-478-0556

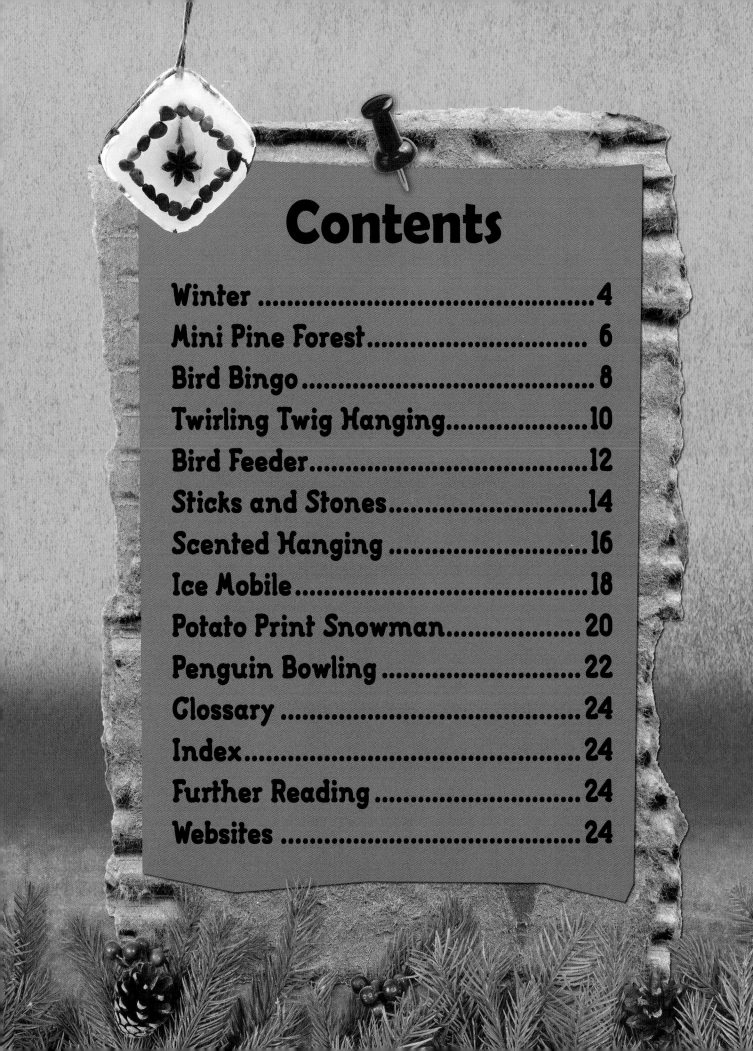

Contents

WINTER

Winter is one of the seasons of the year. The months of winter are December, January and February.

Winter is the coldest season of the year. It also has the smallest amount of daylight. Most winter trees are completely bare, as all their leaves have fallen to the ground during the autumn months. You are more likely to see hail, frost and even snow. But don't let that stop you from going outside and enjoying the winter landscape.

Snow is just one of the fun things about winter. You can build snowmen, go sledding and even make snow angels. Winter might be cold, with all of the animals snuggled up and hibernating, but there is still much to do and see!

This book will guide you to all the great natural materials you can collect. Bring them back home and discover what great craft projects you can make in the comfort of your warm home.

Whatever you find, always remember to ask a grown up before you pick it up. A good rule to remember is to collect only what has fallen from plants or trees and never pick anything that is still alive or growing. Always remember to wash your findings before you use them.

5

Mini Pine Forest

One of the only tree that stays green all through the winter is the pine tree. It has needles instead of leaves. Make your own mini pine forest using cuttings from larger trees.

You will need:

- Pine tree cuttings
- Modeling clay
- Plastic lid
- Glue
- Paintbrush
- Flour
- Colored card stock
- Scissors
- Pencil

1

Press down some modeling clay in a plastic lid.

If you can't find any pine tree cuttings, you can use some twigs, making it look like a lovely, bare, wintry forest.

2

Lightly coat each pine cutting with some glue. Sprinkle some flour over the glue and shake the excess off.

3

Press the pine cuttings into the modeling clay.

4

Fold a piece of colored card stock in half and cut out a teardrop shape.

5

Keep the paper folded and make a small cut at the top to make the wings. Draw the bird's details using a pencil. Decorate your trees with lots of colored birds.

Bird Bingo

If you are quiet and still, you can spot lots of different species of birds. You can turn your bird-spotting into a game of bingo. Just cover the bird you have spotted with a counter and when you have spotted all the birds on your card, just shout BINGO! Only don't shout too loudly or you will scare the birds away.

You will need:
- Paper
- Ruler
- colored pens or pencils
- colored card stock
- Scissors

1

Fold your piece of paper to create six sections. Draw the dividing lines using a pen and a ruler.

2

Draw one bird into each of the six sections.

3

Color in the birds using colored pencils.

4

Make some counters by cutting six squares of colored card stock that fit on the bird squares.

Not all birds stay with us throughout the winter, so check before you draw them on your card. We have included a robin, a sparrow, a dove, a chaffinch and a blackbird on our bingo card.

Twirling Twig Hanging

Nature is often quite bare in the winter. Why not try this craft to brighten up your garden or even your room? Use twigs you have collected from a wintry walk and decorate your hanging with shiny beads.

You will need:
- Twigs
- String
- Beads
- Scissors

Choose four short twigs, four medium twigs and four long ones.

Make three squares by tying each of the four twigs of the same length together at each corner.

3 Tie all three squares together using one long piece of string.

4 Thread beads onto short pieces of string and attach them to the squares.

5 Tie a loop of string to the top of your hanging, and hang it up in the garden or your room.

Bird Feeder

It is harder for birds to find food and keep warm in the winter. You can help by making this simple bird feeder using a pinecone you have collected on one of your walks.

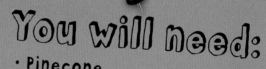

You will need:

- Pinecone
- Lard
- Bird seed
- String
- Scissors
- Plate
- Butter knife

1 Tie some string around the top of the pine cone.

2 Press the lard into the pine cone using a butter knife.

3

Put your bird seed onto a plate.

4

Roll the pine cone in the seed mix to cover it evenly.

There are many different types of bird feeders you can make. Look out for more designs so you can feed as many birds as possible.

Sticks and Stones

You may be tempted to stay inside during winter, but you'll be surprised how much fun you can have in the frost and snow! This simple and fun game can be made and played when you venture outside.

You will need:
- sticks
- stones
- string
- scissors
- correction fluid

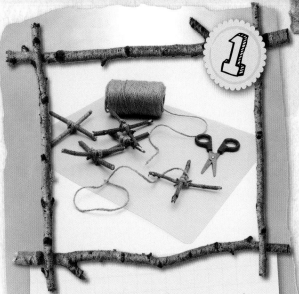

Tie two twigs together with string, in the shape of a cross. Make five of these in total.

Find five large, flat stones and draw a large circle on each of them with correction fluid.

3 Make the grid using the four long sticks.

4 Use correction fluid to draw a line on the other side of one stone.

How to play:
This is a simple game of tic-tac-toe. Use the stone with the circle and line to flip and see who goes first. One person uses the stones and the other uses the sticks.

Scented Hanging

Winter has its own smells and scents. When you are outside, notice how crisp frosty mornings or pine forests smell. But it's not just the outdoors – some fruit and spices remind us of winter, too. This simple hanging craft will spread a lovely wintry scent in your home.

You will need:

- Ribbon
- Slice of dried orange
- cloves
- cinnamon stick
- Sprig of holly
- Glue
- Scissors
- Three red beads

1

Tie a long piece of ribbon through the slice of the dried orange.

2

Press some cloves into the orange slice.

3

Tie a cinnamon stick to the top of the orange slice using the ribbon.

4

Using glue, stick two holly leaves and the red beads onto the cinnamon sticks.

5

Tie the ribbon into a bow, so you can hang it up.

Ask an adult to help you dry your own orange by cutting an orange into slices and baking them at 125 degrees for 2-3 hours, turning them occasionally.

17

Ice Mobiles

Winter is usually very cold and some nights it can be below freezing. Make the most of the frigid temperatures by making a really cool ice sculpture that you can hang outside!

You will need:

- Plastic container
- String
- Pebbles
- Sticks
- Aniseed star
- Scissors

1 In a plastic container, make a pattern out of some pebbles, sticks and an aniseed star.

Try using unusual jelly molds to create fun shapes for your ice mobiles.

2 Tie a knot in a length of string and place it in the plastic container. You may want to secure it in place with tape.

3

Fill the plastic container with water, so it covers the pebbles.

4

Put the container in the freezer until it has frozen. If it is a really cold night, you can try leaving it outside.

5

Take the ice block out of the container and hang it up outside.

Potato Print Snowman

Snow can melt really quickly when the sun starts to shine again. Make it last a little longer by making a printed snowman with potatoes and twigs you have gathered.

You will need:

- Potato
- White, brown, orange and black paint
- Blue card
- Plate or paint palette
- Twigs
- Pencil

1

Ask an adult to cut a potato in half.

2

Spread white paint on the cut surface of each potato half. Use the halves to print the head and body of the snowman.

Use twigs to print some arms with brown paint.

Using some black paint, use the top and bottom side of a pencil to print the face.

Spread some orange paint on a small stick to print the nose. You can use your fingertip and some white paint to print snow.

21

Penguin Bowling

Penguins live in the Arctic, where it's winter all year round! You can make your own feathered friends and play for hours with this fun skittles game.

You will need:

- 10 small yogurt drink containers
- Black, yellow and orange card stock
- Googly eyes
- Scissors
- Glue
- Tape

1 Cut a strip of black card stock the height of the drink container. This will make the head and body of the penguin.

2 Fold the card in half and cut a B shape out. Then wrap the card around the drink container and fasten it with sticky tape.

22

3

Cut two U shapes out of black card to make wings. Glue them to the side of the penguin body.

4

Cut out orange feet and stick them to the bottom of the body. Glue on googly eyes.

5

Cut out two yellow triangles, fold them in half and stick them onto the head to form the beak. Make another nine penguins!

Glossary

bowling (BOH-ling) A game that involves rolling a ball toward pins in order to knock as many of them down as possible.

frost (FROST) Powdery ice that forms on things in freezing weather.

gather (GATH-ur) To collect.

hail (HAYL) Pellets of frozen rain that fall in showers.

hibernate (HY-bur-nayt) When an animal goes to sleep for the winter.

pine (PYN) A tree that has needles instead of leaves and stays green in the winter; pine trees are used to celebrate Christmas.

Index

Further Reading

Appleby, Alex. *What Happens in Winter? Four Super Seasons.* New York: Gareth Stevens, 2014.

Barnham, Kay. *Winter. Seasons.* New York: PowerKids Press, 2010.

Owen, Ruth. *Holiday Crafts.* New York: PowerKids Press, 2013.

Websites

For web resources related to the subject of this book, go to: www.windmillbooks.com/weblinks and select this book's title.